A Little Excitement

A Little Excitement

Poems by

Nancy Scott

Cover design by Shay Culligan
Cover art by Nancy Scott

ISBN: 978-1-952326-73-8

Kelsay Books
502 South 1040 East, A-119
American Fork, Utah, 84003

for Peter

Acknowledgments

These poems, some in slightly different forms, appeared in the following books and journals.

A Siege of Raptors: "Rabbit Diva"

Caduceus: "Mixed Greens"

Cyclamens & Swords: "The Red Leash," "Some Things Never Change," and "Time Is of the Essence"

Journal of New Jersey Poets: "Eating Chocolate"

Kelsey Review: "The Birds," "When the Sun Breaks," and "The Whistler"

Mad Poets' Review: "Death Attends a Poetry Reading"

Pudding Magazine: "The Parade"

Qarrtsiluni: "Limits"

The Raven Chronicles: "The Elephant in England"

Rufous Salon: "The Old Woman at the End of the Block"

Segue: "My Nightmares Are Like That"

Shot Glass Journal: "Keeping in Touch," "Refusing to Mark the Event Insignificant," and "Things"

The Owl Prince: "The Scrawny Chicken"

Umbrella: "Still Life with Dead Rabbit and Flugelhorn"

U.S.1 Worksheets: "Paradise," "The Poor Man's Bride," "Burnt Toast," and "A Little Excitement"

Verse Wisconsin: "The Elephant in England"

Contents

Part III Dumping the Emu

Part I

Into the Wild

The Parade

The War comes. We hear artillery across the river;
    flares light the night sky, buildings shake,
but bombs never reach us. We go about our lives
    pretending that nothing has changed.
We visit the coffee shop, watch a packed bus
    veer around the line outside a bakery.
The dogs look hungrier. Women push prams,
    children play in the park, bars stay open late.

One day Bim and I are sitting on a low wall outside
    our apartment when an elephant plods by,
a giraffe swinging its long neck, then a grizzly
    with her cubs followed by a zebra, a gazelle,
and a monkey on stilts bringing up the rear.

A colonel in full regalia on a great stallion
    gallops to the head of the group. He blows
his whistle three times. The animals halt
    with military precision, except for the cubs.
Lured by the smell of fresh fish, they cut out,
    head for the vendor's stall. When they hear
the whistle again, they scramble back in line.
    The crowd applauds.

(more)

I know this sounds implausible: an orderly group
    of wild animals. A hallucination? Perhaps
the air we breathe is compromised, the chimney
    sweep dislodging toxic soot and ash.
What's the alternative? Homes in rubble, bodies
    piled up, blood pooling in the streets?
No, this is what we witnessed.

Now the colonel stops, inspects his troops, nudges
    the gazelle into formation with his crop,
then leads them onto the Causeway and out of sight.
    Lone sedan speeds past. The street quiets.

A Little Excitement

I know what I know, that's about it.
Yesterday was one of those lovely days,
the forsythia furious with yellow.
It lined the busy boulevard that stretches
between two cloverleafs. A misnomer!
Those cloverleafs are not green nor can they
be examined like I did as a child, grass stains
on my knees, my nose close to the ground
searching for a four-leaf one to bring me
good luck. I've learned that luck is an illusion
that keeps us from going mad.

Today, my car hydroplaned off the boulevard,
landed in a ditch. Fortunately, I wasn't hurt.
A helicopter hovered overhead, attempted
to land in a soccer field. Swirling dust routed
the hapless children in every direction.
A bewildered coyote with an injured paw
was snarling traffic. Cars honked.
The coyote kept zigzagging across lanes.
Another coyote joined the first.
They walked upright now, slapping
each other's back before suddenly vanishing.

The Bear

Anatoly, a Jewish émigré, tells me
a Russian joke in broken English,
over pizza. I nod between mouthfuls
comprehending nothing
except the bear.
When he said he'd left Minsk,
via Canada, to work in the USA,
no endless wait for a visa, no costly bribes,
I had trouble understanding,
just like I can't follow the joke
about the bear. A great furry paw
whacks Anatoly's head, sends his punch line
dangling from a creaky ceiling fan.
Anatoly shakes his fist at the bear
who ruined his joke.
I swear it was the other way around.

The Birds

Consider my neighbor Pete
who calls to birds in a hundred voices.
He's tracked them from Canada
to Tahiti to the Galapagos Islands.

The whole family speaks *bird*.
His daughter sports feathers
in her hair; his son, a nose like a beak.
From the privacy of my shaded window,
I've seen his wife flap her arms and screech.

I'd like to keep to myself but his wife
flutters about my front door
bringing tins of freshly-baked cookies
peppered with seeds.
What a delight, so warm and so crunchy.

Refusing to Mark the Event Insignificant

Once there was a scourge
that blanched the waters of Lake Michigan.
It transformed the Loop into a solo heartbeat,
except for a twelve-toed priest, fleeing.

It robbed the stolid General of his armor,
electrified the steel at Navy Pier.
It chiseled limestone blocks along the Point
into a multitude of feet.

I can still see a blizzard turning
Wacker Drive into a rout of taillights,
while white feathers bloomed
in the snow along The Magnificent Mile.

Paradise

A waif-like creature with long dark hair
and piercing eyes walked into
a cafe on the upper West Side, ordered
double espresso and a bear claw.

"Do you mind?" She slipped into a chair
across from me. "I'm Paradise," she said.
I said, "What an unusual name."
She broke off a chunk of bear claw
and popped it into her mouth. "I'm always hungry.
I think I've got a second stomach."

That afternoon, I ran into Paradise
wolfing a burger, asked her where she was from.
"I'm not sure," she said. "Sometimes
I think I'm from Alabama, but then I get this image
of snow. Maybe I'm from a place that's cold."
She crinkled her nose.

"I'd love to hang out and hear more," I said,
"but I have to pick up my daughter from dance class."
"Your daughter's lucky to have a mom,"
Paradise said. "I must have one somewhere,
but I'm not sure I can find her."

A week went by. I grew impatient
to see Paradise. Imagine my shock—
she'd shaved her head.
"I sold my hair to a wigmaker," she said.
"I needed the money." She pirouetted right there

(more)

on the sidewalk. "And, there's more…" She did
a soft shoe shuffle around the telephone pole.
"I've landed the part of a gamine in a snuff film."

Alarmed, I said, "You know how that ends?"
"For sure," Paradise said. "I've done it
twelve times and here I am!"

Into the Wild

She was in the woods digging
when she came upon
a cache of dreams.

She spread them out
on a pile of dead leaves
carefully detaching
one dream from the other.

A nascent dream quivered
its transparent wings
attempted to fly
but faltered.
Watch me, she said.

She stood on her toes
pressed her face to the wind
swooped and floated
floated and rose
over the treetops
the roofs, the mountains

until she could feel
her bones dissolve
and the dream
slipped alongside her.

Together they soared
shapeless as memory
straying farther and farther
into the wild.

Gone Fishing

I was deep into this dream
where our tangled bodies
were naked in the wet grass,
stars overhead, suddenly
a neon sign flashed,
Vegan Cocktail Guaranteed to...,
no matter, the magic was gone.
I floundered around for
a new dream and found myself
standing in front of your grave,
but you weren't there.
Gone Fishing was staked
next to your headstone.
I know how much you hate fish,
so what changed your mind?
It turned to autumn overnight;
yesterday the forsythia
were blooming, but today
I'm shuffling through fallen
leaves trying to find you.
No one remembers seeing you
or a fishing pole slung over
your shoulder, so here's the deal:
If I scroll to the part where we
were throbbing with passion,
would you forget all
this craziness and come back?

Some Things Never Change

My mind lives in a neighborhood I don't want to visit.
No one speaks the same language.
What passes for civility
is simply lack of clarity.
I never know who carries a switchblade
or a Glock. I hope a bag of potatoes
is just that, not another IED designed to blow me
to smithereens, and the voices in my head
are real people on TV next door.
Days turn in too early.
Nights carry on too long. Tick, tock.
I rarely go out anymore.
Rooms are cluttered with ideas
gone wrong. I want to make a chicken sandwich
but I forgot to buy the chicken and I've got no bread.
No matter, I can do without until the tracks of my mind
finally rewind: I'll answer the doorbell
dressed in bridal white,
a gardenia at my ear, and you'll be waiting to lead me
down the garden path the way you always have.

Death Attends a Poetry Reading

He sets his shabby book-bag
on the floor, slips into the seat
beside me, pinning me against
the wall, then turns and smiles,
his brow a well-traveled map,
thick blunt fingers splayed
across his thighs.
Like an arch wind, his sweet
breath whips around the room,
riffles book pages, rags on
the speaker's words, spilling
them in corners, swirling
them like grain.
Inches from my shoulder,
he leans as if to whisper.
Silence—no applause.

Mixed Greens

After a spate of relatives dying, funeral wreaths, heels
sticking in mud on the way to the gravesite,
I decided to dine with Death to discuss the situation.
I love what you're wearing, said Death to jump-start
the conversation.
Hand-screened poppies on silk, I said. *Are you partial to red?*
I'm color blind, said Death.
Once, I turned a few heads in this dress.
I remember. Death smiled as he signaled the waiter.
He ordered the juiciest rib on a standing rib roast, grilled root
vegetables, and pricey Bordeaux for himself.
The lady will have mixed greens.
Sensing my displeasure, he explained it like this:
Do you think I'll be free for dinner forever?
No, I said.
Do you sit all day in front of a computer?
Yes, I said.
He slathered butter on a crescent roll.
Never lift a finger to exercise?
True, I said.
And those Big Macs and fries you love so much?
I hung my head.
You'll thank me later, said Death.

Keeping in Touch

I heard from my father.

If he were still alive, he'd be 95
on his next birthday in July.

He congratulated me on my new book,
poems about my childhood.

You've been unfair to your mother, he said.
She couldn't help herself, but I did love her.

You were always fighting, I said.

Such a long time ago, it's grown blurry.

*****

It rained the entire afternoon.

I spent an hour detangling the philodendron.

I thought about Mother.

After she died, her voice circled endlessly
on my answering machine.

What are you cooking for dinner tonight?

Playing Chess with the Muskrat

It's four a.m. I can't sleep. I'm playing chess
with the Muskrat. He's beating me.
"Hey, kiddo," I say, "I know you moved
the bishop when you thought I wasn't looking."
"Hey, insomniac, you got someone else
to keep you company?"
"Careful, Muskrat. I remember the jacket
my mother had made out of your kin."
"Yeah, yeah," the Muskrat says. "Let's play."

I think of all those furs I coveted as a kid.
My mother's foxes—hard, beady eyes, sharp
nails—draped around her neck. Nobody messed
with my mother with, or without, the foxes.
I don't mention her silky Russian sable,
the chinchilla, three-quarter curly Persian lamb
and matching hat, or full-length mink
I had remodeled so it fits me now.

"Sorry Muskrat, life's too short. Checkmate."

The Boy with Ice Eyes

for Jimmy

Death was hungry, needed a fix,
watched the boy with ice eyes
drive a '64 Mustang up Potrero Hill.

Death growled, *It's getting late,*
as the Mustang hovered ready to fly
down the other side of the hill.

The boy's foot hit the gas,
Death lunged, snatched the brake hoses.
The Mustang careened at 55 mph
straight for the traffic on Third.

His ice eyes took aim to make the turn,
hands steady, the boy rammed
the Mustang into the granite wall
of the United Methodist Church.

KABOOM

All Hell broke loose.
Angels on duty that night
took after Death with a Flying Wedge.
Time froze, owls gasped,
the moon scooted behind the church spire.

The boy climbed out
of the demolished car
without a scratch.

Death shook off dirt from Potrero Hill,
looked at the car, looked at the boy,
spat out a feather.

Part II

The Lost Sheep

Timing Is of the Essence

I love the way you're always late. Gives me time
to finish the revision, stack plates, take a razor to my legs.
Just come in; you don't have to knock.
I love the way you're always on time by your accounting.
I helped a guy fix his flat tire. Or, *I stopped to buy you these…*
The way you slouch against the wall, puzzling what
I've said, your hair mussed—it's a windy day.
And tickets in the envelope, giveaways where one of us
was the 13th caller. *Should we take in a movie or stay?*
I love our acrobatics, the scratchiness of your mustache,
our bodies slick with sweat. How we laughed
when the thunder rumbled
as if the gods had given their approval…or not.
Alone at 3 a.m. with a ticking clock—our glory time has passed.

Eating Chocolate

And these are a few of my other vices:
envy, impatience, ice cream drumsticks,
ability to overlook clutter and resist temptation
to straighten it up, a pain in the chest that isn't pain
but something like longing—any warm body
next to me, the taste of salt on his skin—
dreams fashioned by never arriving, distracted
by people who don't appear and won't let go.
I wear on my sleeve a heart that beats
to its own irascible rhythm.

Things

after Borges

My laptop, ledgers,
weekly calendar, photos
and stack of notes
I've not responded to.

Artwork, planters,
Afghan rugs,
each with its own story,
unforgettable, but forgotten
when I'm gone.

Many things—
French country table,
antique cherry cupboard,
opal brooch,
tea-stained letter
from Jakarta.

At my bedside,
a white ceramic lamp,
its luminosity
holding back the night.
All so fickle and so fine!

They'll outlast me
and not care a wit
about my demise.

The Old Woman at the End of the Block

I was running out of time,
so decided to pay a visit
to the 103-year-old woman
who lived at the end of the block.
With measuring cup in hand,
I rang the doorbell, and asked,
Could you spare a year or two?
She invited me in for tea
and, while pouring Oolong
into chipped porcelain, she said,
I could give up 1923.
It wasn't a good year for me.
She hesitated.
No, I'll give you 1972 instead,
a stellar year. You look as if
you could use some luck.
We were chatting about the weather
and such, when she leaned over
and whispered,
If you still need more time,
come see me again,
because after I'm dead,
what good is it then?
I thanked her profusely,
and, with cup filled to the brim,
I took my sweet time home.

Sighting at a Charity Sale of Zimbabwe Sculpture

for Avery Brooks

The shop was deserted except for two elderly
volunteers chatting, and me. I was browsing hippos
and fish when a tall dark man entered

in a jogging suit, bald head sleek as polished ebony.
He began rushing about pointing to sculptures.
One volunteer trailed with paper and pen; the other

had an uneasy grin as if she wanted to dial 911.
After he'd paid and left, an audible sigh spread through
the shop. Stroking a serpentine bird, I couldn't resist,

*Don't you recognize him? He's the Emissary
who battled the Dominion and imprisoned
pah-wraiths in the fire caves.*

Visibly paler, the old ladies stared at me.
Perhaps I should have reassured them
I'd not beamed down from some alien planet,

but I motioned with my hand to gather them
closer and whispered, *And he guarded
Alpha Quadrant from Bajoran wormhole invaders.*

They scurried to the window just in time to see
the Starfleet Commander of Deep Space Nine
take off in a celestial blue Odyssey.

Animal Planters

It was freezing today at the flea market,
not much for sale, not a cent on me.
With checkbook, it's never too cold to haggle.
I bought an elephant, foot nudging a blue ball,
ears flared, trunk curled upward in triumph.

As for animal planters, I've no willpower.
My shelves are lined: three kittens in shoe,
grinning bear on log, koala hugging tree,
Not to mention cocker spaniel under mailbox.
buck-toothed rabbit or kangaroo,
ponies, swans, dogs, donkeys, ducks,
two deer, fawn and doe intertwined,
green stallion flying, red fox, and a blue goose
with a polka-dot kerchief.

Last week as I lingered at his booth, a seller asks,
Aren't you the lady who bought a wood duck?
Oh, you remembered, I answer to save time
from haggling over two planter/bookends,
magnificent rams' heads, though
I couldn't say which of the ducks he meant.

I've found them from Montreal to Santa Fe,
in Boston's antique shops, dusty barns in Ohio.
I grieve for the overpriced cockatoo in Canton,
slightly chipped panther left behind.
Thousands wait to be saved from the dumpster.
It's only a matter of shelf space and stamina.
I can't stop.
I've become the SPCA for animal planters.

Simon Says in the Shopping Mall

The Easter Bunny is white fluff
with a blue velveteen coat and glasses askew.
He's old, Leah whispers.
Bunnies get old too, I say.
Can I talk to him?
You can try.

Leah bounds over to where he sits
surrounded by green and white latticework,
asks something I can't hear, then runs back.
He told me he's got five bunnies in his family.
But he can't talk, I remind her.
She gives me that look that means—
Get with the program.

Then Leah's playing a game
with her furry friend.
Simon says, touch your head.
Simon says, touch your knees.
Now touch your shoulders.
Each time the Easter Bunny gets it right.

See, HE listens to me, she says,
which coming from a four-year-old
sounds very much like accusation.

The Lost Sheep

That afternoon when the farmer arrived
at the pasture to check on his sheep,
he discovered they'd all disappeared.
To make sure, he blinked. No sheep;
instead a bustling town
where people scurried in and out of shops,
cars honked. Football game
in the new stadium. What a madhouse!
The farmer went home to tell his wife.
"Our sheep are gone," he said.
"Oh my," she said and went back to her sweeping.
"They've disappeared," he said more loudly.
"Don't yell at me," she said. "I'm thinking."
The farmer grew more agitated.
"How will we live with no wool to sell?"
"You could paint pictures of sheep,"
she said finally. "It would be easier than
all that shearing and carding and spinning.
And no more sheep dip."
"I don't know how to paint," the farmer wailed.
"Just splash a lot of green and white
on each canvas," said his wife, "and call them
'Sheep Grazing in a Pasture.'
Some fool will insist you're a genius
and people will flock to buy your work."

The Faltering Muse

Ragdale, Lake Forest, IL

An angel, hand-carved in Italy,
shipped here by mistake.

The artist insists there is no angel;
yet a large wooden statue,
face snaggled by the elements,
clings to the studio's south wall.

One afternoon, I wander out to the studio,
feel the angel softly shift;
perhaps prairie winds casting shadows.

Inside, blank canvas fills the wall.
The artist, perched on a spattered stool,
explains his concept for self-portrait:

The angles are so complex, he says,
it could take months to get it right.

His vanity requires no response.
A steady rain begins to fall.
As I slosh beneath the dripping angel,
I hear it groan.

Rabbit Diva

She was the warm-up for Wayne Newton
in Vegas. She had a million-dollar fur coat
and pink ears to kill for. Who knows what
her talent was—clearly not vocal. Maybe
hopping out of a top hat with nothing on
but bunny fur. Whatever it was drove
the audience wild. They booed Newton
off the stage, then hooted and clapped
until she appeared for an encore.
Next day, she was replaced by a clown act.
Nobody upstages Wayne Newton.
Leaving Vegas behind, she reinvented
herself as The Rabbit Diva of eBay, hawking
Newton memorabilia—no hard feelings—
bunny lockets, bunny rings, and life-sized
inflatables of Jessica *I'm not bad* Rabbit.

Still Life with Dead Rabbit and Flugelhorn

Dear Artist,

Though your work is rendered with exquisite
detail, we were not convinced that is a trout

on the pewter plate, but rather a catfish,
with all those whiskers. Is the three-tined

fork suspended in mid-air over the fish
meant to titillate our taste buds?

The symbolism of six long-stemmed roses
stuck in the wedge of Stilton and shamrocks

floating out of the donkey's mouth eludes us.
After closely examining the painting,

we are unable to find either the dead rabbit
or the flugelhorn, which, by the way, no one

plays anymore. The window painted black
resting on an easel dominates the work.

Consider a new title:
Window Painted Black Resting on an Easel.

Get rid of everything else, then line up
five clementines to balance the palette.

The Art Exhibit Will End on December 32nd

headline from Princeton online, Arts and Culture, 2010

Actually, the exhibit at the Swallow Gallery opened
and closed the same day. The police had to be called

to control the crowds trying to enter the gallery.
Featured was the work of foodie artist, Sherry Sorbay,

who has received national acclaim for her edible collages.
The lucky ones who made it into the gallery oohed

and aahed while free wine flowed. Then they dismantled
the art: cheddar cubes, grapes, hummus with olives,

followed by broccoli quiche and herb-roasted squab.
For dessert, they gravitated en masse to the north wall

of the gallery for lemon chiffon pie and raspberry tarts.
That food was cardboard cutouts proved to be no problem.

Several guests commented that supermarket varieties
are often tougher and more bland. Within a hour, nothing

was left, except crumbled napkins and frilly toothpicks.
The January exhibit will feature the work of Sicilian

collagist Sal Sarosa known for his stuffed mussels
and sumptuous meat dish, *farsu magru,* with melanzane.

Burnt Toast

You could adjust the lever on the toaster, we suggested,
believing our earnestness might persuade Ellen to do just that.
You're right, she agreed as she scraped the burnt off today's
cold toast, charred bits littering the floor like dead bugs.

When Bliss and I arrived at her cabin on one of the Finger Lakes,
Ellen invited us to stay as long as we liked, but insisted on
doing the cooking. To avoid being rude, we ate the burnt toast
and the mystery stew she simmered for hours.

Bliss is a vegetarian so he assumed that whatever was in
that stew came from Ellen's garden. One drizzly morning,
she swept up the bugs, put on Wellingtons and a poncho,
said, *going to check the traps.* First time she mentioned that.

Bliss rolled his eyes, but we kept silent—better not to ask
what she hoped to snare. Since Ellen worked in town,
for two months we slept in, got high, and sometimes walked
along the lake until even awesome scenery became an eyesore.

Worse yet, our stash was nearly gone. The idea that Bliss and I
might be eating possum or skunk or god-knows-what convinced
us it was time to leave. That night, thankfully no stew—the traps
must have been empty—we told Ellen we landed a gig

in Buffalo. Next day she handed us a loaf of freshly baked bread,
yeasty and warm. *Safe travel,* she said. We trekked miles
to the highway. No idea which way to head, we unwrapped
the bread and ate the whole loaf, every crumb.

Part III

Dumping the Emu

Brief Bio

I was Playmate of the Month in 1964,
theater critic for the *San Francisco Examiner,*
Texas singer and songwriter for over 30 years,
teacher of the deaf, weaver, poet, pediatrician,
researcher, and art historian.
I wrote a book about cruising
the Virgin Islands, ran a health clinic in Zambia.
I've been married several times,
currently to Dave. We live on a bluff
overlooking Lake Hamilton.
Years ago, I wed Thomas, a burglar,
while he was still in prison.
I've produced many children,
going back to the 1700s. I lived a full life,
and died in 2003, according to Google.

The Whistler

A young man came to rent a room.
He told me he had no job, no money.
How do you live? I asked.
I barter, he replied. *I bet
You'd like a widescreen TV.*
I shook my head.
Perhaps a new refrigerator?
I'd like the rent in cash.
A year's supply of frozen meat?
I'm a vegetarian.
He rapped his knuckles on the door,
I'll be back, he said,
and bounded down the front steps,
whistling.

Locking Horns

At seventeen, I got Mother's permission
to chose the décor for my bedroom.
It hardly mattered
because I was on my way to college.
Pink, she said.
Maroon and lime, I made clear
to Mr. Ralph, her decorator
—how Mother could think of me
as she rattled around the empty house.

Then it was my hair—thick, dark,
parted in the middle, hanging straight.
You look like an Indian, Mother said.
I reminded her I'd worn it parted
with braids when I was a kid.
You weren't looking for a husband.

How excited she was to meet the PhD
I was about to marry.
Having traveled three thousand miles
to the wedding, Mother was furious
when she saw the black cocktail suit
instead of a wedding dress.
We go to a lot of parties, I explained.
It's bad luck, she insisted.

Twenty-six years later when I told her
we were getting divorced, she said,
I warned you not to get married in black.

When the Sun Breaks

I am the whisper behind you
in the check-out line at the mall.
I am the riffle of pages
in Michael Crichton's last novel.
Sometimes I'm the crush in the aisle
on the 8:15 to New York,
flash of blonde hair past the window
when your Subaru decides to stall,
or sultry air rushing to fill
space left by a familiar smell.
I'm not the cause of night fevers,
but rather the shape of your dream.
I'll wait for you when the sun breaks
over Our Lady of Sorrows.
Don't wait on the steps. Come in.
I've prepared for your arrival—
almond torte stippled with honey,
Zinfandel fruity and rich.
The kids are all at camp
and Rover's at the vet's.

The Poor Man's Bride

Penniless, he built his bride
a house with no roof or walls,
only a door of twisted twigs.

Most days, she'd sit and stare
across the foggy moor, dream
of children she would never rear.

At night, she'd hook a kettle
on the hob that didn't warm
and latch the door against the wind.

A wild dog adopted her.
She'd pluck the burrs from its coat
and feed it off her plate.

She never raised her voice
to complain, yet the poor man knew
that howling from the uplands

would rouse in her
desires he could not fulfill.
The day she disappeared

she left his supper on the table,
a brackish stew
of thistledown and thorns.

What She Couldn't Stay Away From

In a suite on the sixteenth floor
of the seaside resort, he flung her
with such force she crashed into
the far end of the spectrum.

Violet prisms starlit her brain.
She bartered secrets with an indigo snake
at a rest stop in Texas, braided
wild-blue-yonder roses into her hair,

roamed the chaparral
with a green-tailed towhee.
She stooped to pluck buttercups
and gave them to a blind coyote.

In the zebra lounge of the seaside resort,
her limber fingers ran an arpeggio
up and down an orange piano.
He paced the suite on the sixteenth floor,

whined his teeth had grown numb waiting.
He'd laid out a gown of scarlet organza.
She slid the silk over her long buff body
sounding the depths of his desire.

The Elephant in England

The beast which passeth all others in wite and mind...
—Aristotle

I'm the fifth cousin of Babar's wife, Celeste.
We elephants keep track of our lineages.

She invited me on holiday in London, where
we tromped from Hampstead to Kensington.

You can have the city and all its amenities.
Not a single mud hole in sight. I got arrested

sloshing about in the Serpentine with a bevy
of native ducks, then got sent off to Whipsnade,

where I've become eye candy for tourists.
I've got all the plants, roots, and bark I can eat,

good packing mud, too, though Babar has never
bothered to visit. Truth is, every elephant

knows the fool married above his station.
Now my teeth are nearly ground down and I'm sick

of the stench of humans. I want to return to Africa
where I can smell the sweet grasses again.

Noodle Doctor

I visited a Chinese noodle doctor.
She examined me with chopsticks
and declared my edible parts overcooked.

Is there a cure?
She shook her head.
Can't you do anything?

She ripped open her starched white coat,
a rooster tattooed on her breast.
She stretched her neck to crow,

tangled with the hanging plants,
and nearly choked to death.

Dumping the Emu

from a MSNBC news report, 2009

Here's something to think about:
the Yuwaalaraay believe the sun was created
when someone tossed an emu egg into the sky.

If you happen to travel through Mississippi,
near the city of Forest, make a wide swath
around errant emus. Leave their capture

to law enforcement. They'll come with Tasers
and handcuffs and take into custody
one of the few flightless birds on this planet.

The female of the species is notorious.
She'll leave a dozen eggs for one male
to turn over in the nest ten times a day—

for weeks—and then care for her chicks,
while she seduces the next fool.
No wonder there's a half-crazed emu
dodging traffic on Interstate 20.

What Is Meant to Be

Since we cannot meet in this world,
we agree to meet in *Shattered* on page 167,
four chapters after we kissed good-bye.
Months before, we were convinced
we'd be together again, the way young lovers
insist it was meant to be, but until this day in June,
it had all been dreams. I knew you'd return
from Ohio someday and I'd be on a date
with a guy I'm about to break-up with
because he isn't you. I'd asked him to drive me home
where I recognize your blue sedan parked
across the street. I tell the guy I'm with I can't see him
anymore. When he asks why, I put my finger to his lips,
kiss him on the cheek, and tell him it's not his fault.
Heart pounding, I hesitate to approach your car
only to find that you're still a dream.
Instead, I slip my key into the front door lock.
When the wind suddenly kicks up,
I feel someone behind me, whispering
my name. I can't move. What if…

Nightmares

after The Empire of Light, II
by Rene Magritte, oil on canvas, 1950s

My nightmares are like that—
a single street lamp, not illuminating anything,
the street's bathed in darkness, and I'm running
and stumble, and there's a house, maybe two,
maybe three, I lose count as I'm running,
out of breath now, and light from a window, here
and there, but the street is deserted, no people,
no cars, not even a stray cat, and yet behind
one of those closed doors may be what I'm trying
to reach, but I can't stop to find out, so I keep
on running, and will myself not to look up,
because over the trees, above this desolate street,
there's a bright blue sky frothy with clouds, and
if I could get a good running start, I could lift off
and soar, leave this endless street where no one
goes out, not for a smoke or to walk their dog,
and if I stay steady, I could float forever
in perpetual day, but I know that's not what I am
looking for, so if I can reach the corner,
I've got a hunch that on the next street, day is
day and night's night, and with my legs aching,
I'd settle for that, so I keep on running, past
the same windows, same trees, still hopeful
I'll make it, because as I said at the start,
my nightmares are like that.

The Red Leash

Sometimes I say I have to take my dog for a walk—
even though I have no dog—just because it's such
an ordinary thing to say. I've always thought so
ever since I had a black Lab who constantly

scratched at the door to go out. Today I walked
up and down the same path in the park expecting
someone to ask if I was looking for my dog
but the park was empty, the ground blanketed

in ocher and burnt umber, leaves not caring a fig
about my dog so I left and went into a pet shop
where I bought a red leash. When the clerk asked
what breed it was for, I said, *a black Lab*

while a caramel and crème Shih Zhu
with enormous eyes stared at me from its cage
like it knew I was a dog lover but needy of a dog
to walk on that lead. As it crossed my mind to buy

that Shih Zhu, a child pointed and said, *Mommy,*
I want that one, and the fickle dog, tail wagging,
licked the child's fingers poking through
the wire mesh and forgot all about me.

Limits

after Borges

Of these streets full of potholes, there's more
than one where I've blown out my tires,
and knowing it, I blame the politicians,
who, always on the verge of losing

the next election, don't care to make
my ride a smooth one. So many politicians
with no limits, who in this country have we,
unknowingly, said goodbye to for good?

As the next election nears, and claims,
counterclaims, and smears leave only
bitterness to savor, is there, perchance, just one
who will emerge and surprise us?

With the world in foreclosure, I find detours
at every intersection. Even the guy ahead of me,
turn signal wildly blinking, has a spare tire
mounted on his trunk.

The sturdy grey Corolla is, I fear, the last car
I will own. Not one road will miss us
that I'm sure. I hear a newly paved one
runs past where the burning bushes bloom.

The Scrawny Chicken

Chicken Licken had a hard life.
      She had witnessed bombings and fires
and people dead and wounded in the streets.
      Food was scarce. Somehow, she had managed
to avoid the axe. With all the stress, she had lost
      her lustrous feathers and plump figure.
On that day, when she was pecking for food
      outside a ruined shop, something
fell on her head. It certainly wasn't an acorn.
      Not one tree left standing anywhere. She knew it
was too small to be a missile. Maybe space junk or
      most likely the sky was falling. Whom to tell?
Loosey Goosey, Ducky Lucky, and Turkey Lurky
      had been served up early in the war.
Should she tell the King? No, he was responsible
      for all this devastation. So Chicken Licken
ignored the bump on her head and continued searching
      for scraps to eat. If indeed the sky was falling,
she prayed it would land on the King's head,
      then peace would reign in the kingdom again.

About the Author

Nancy Scott, managing editor of *U.S.1 Worksheets* for more than fourteen years, is a poet, fiction writer, and collage artist. She has had nine books of poetry published since 2007 and over 400 individual poems have appeared in journals and anthologies. Her prize winning collages have been exhibited in juried shows and selected as cover images for several of her own books as well as featured art in print and online journals. Recently, her novels *Marriage by Fire* (2018) and *Shattered* (2019) have received outstanding reviews.

She is a recipient of a Ragdale Fellowship and spent several summers attending Frank Bidart's Master Class in poetry at Skidmore College.

She turned to writing after a long career devoted to social policy issues. She was a social worker for the State of New Jersey responding to allegations of child abuse and neglect and later securing permanent housing for homeless individuals and families. Her experiences were memorialized in *Running Down Broken Cement* (2014). During that time, she was also a foster parent to numerous inner-city teens.

She is a graduate of the University of Chicago and currently resides in Lawrenceville, New Jersey.

www.nancyscott.net
nscott29@aol.com

Other Books by Nancy Scott

Down to the Quick (Plain View Press, 2007)
One Stands Guard, One Sleeps (Plain View Press, 2009)
A Siege of Raptors (Finishing Line Press, 2010)
Detours & Diversions (Main Street Rag, 2011)
On Location (March Street Press, 2011)
Midwestern Memories (Aldrich Press, 2013)
Running Down Broken Cement (Main Street Rag, 2014)
The Owl Prince ((Aldrich Press, 2016)
Ah, Men (Aldrich Press, 2017)
Marriage by Fire (Big Table Publishing Company, 2018)
Shattered (Nancy Scott, publisher, 2019)

www.ingramcontent.com/pod-product-compliance
Lightning Source LLC
Chambersburg PA
CBHW031152090426
42738CB00008B/1296